small
**STEPS**

A TEMPLAR BOOK
First published in the UK in 2009 by Templar Publishing,
an imprint of The Templar Company Limited,
The Granary, North Street, Dorking, Surrey, RH4 1DN
www.templarco.co.uk

Conceived and produced by Weldon Owen Pty Ltd
59–61 Victoria Street, McMahons Point
Sydney NSW 2060, Australia

Copyright © 2009 Weldon Owen Pty Ltd
First published 2009

BONNIER BOOKS
**Group Publisher** John Owen

WELDON OWEN PTY LTD
**Chief Executive Officer** Sheena Coupe
**Creative Director** Sue Burk
**Art Manager** Trucie Henderson
**Senior Vice President, International Sales** Stuart Laurence
**Vice President, Sales: United States and Canada** Amy Kaneko
**Vice President, Sales: Asia and Latin America** Dawn Low
**Administration Manager, International Sales** Kristine Ravn
**Production Manager** Todd Rechner
**Production Coordinators** Lisa Conway, Mike Crowton
**Publishing Coordinator** Gina Belle

**Project Editor** Lesley McFadzean
**Designer** Sarah Norton
**Illustrator** Lloyd Foye

ISBN 978-1-84011-363-1

Colour Reproduction by Chroma Graphics (Overseas) Pte Ltd
Printed by 1010 Printing
Manufactured in China

The paper used in the manufacture of this book is sourced from wood grown in sustainable
forests. It complies with the Environmental Management System Standard ISO 14001:2004

A WELDON OWEN PRODUCTION

# small
# STEPS

Glenn Murphy

templar publishing

# Contents

# Switch off

We all try to switch off lights and appliances when we are not using them. But did you know that when electronic devices are set to standby, they are not really off at all? This picture shows two average homes and their power usage. Look at the electricity metres, and see the difference in monthly power consumption when you make the effort to switch off and unplug.

920 kWh

## Electronic vampires!

When electronic devices continue to suck power from the outlet while left in standby mode, it is called 'standby power' or 'vampire load'. Look how much power these six common household appliances still use when on standby, compared with when they are actually on or in use.

Sound systems can use up to 60%

PCs use up to 29% power on standby

Printers on standby use 25% or more

690 kWh

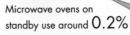

DVD players use around 16%

Televisions use 4% or more

Microwave ovens on standby use around 0.2%

# Keep warm; stay cool

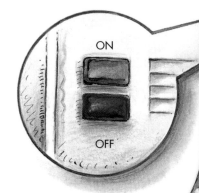

When it gets too cold or too hot indoors, most people turn on the heating or the air-conditioning. But every time they do, they waste energy heating or cooling the whole house, rather than just themselves. You can keep yourself warm or cool – and save energy at the same time – by simply changing your clothes instead.

ON

OFF

## Big energy burners

Heaters and coolers are among the most power-hungry appliances in the house. As you can see, electric heaters and air-conditioners are often hungriest of all, since they burn through electricity very quickly with their red-hot heating elements and spinning fans.

| Wood stove | Gas heater | Electric fan | Electric heater |
|---|---|---|---|
| 0 watts (W) | 80 W | 100 W | 1,000 W |

An air-conditioner uses up to 7,500 W of power cooling a room in summer

...and up to 6,000 W keeping the room warm in winter

**Energy smart**

# Past and present

The world today is burning through a lot more electricity than it did 60 years ago. This is partly because there are a lot more of us here – there are around 2.5 billion more people on the planet today than there were in 1950! But our lifestyles have changed a lot too. With more appliances and gadgets than ever before, homes today use much, much more electricity than they did in 1950.

1950s

## Entertainment

Black-and-white tube televisions used just
**20 W of power**

## Laundry

Twin-tub washing machines used less than
**500 W of power**

## Cooking

Electric cookers and stoves used around
**1,000 W of power**

# TODAY

DVD player
20 W

Plasma TV
340 W

= 390 W

Set top box
30 W

Automatic washing
machine 1,100 W

= 5,500 W

Clothes drier
4,400 W

Electric frying pan
1,200 W

Microwave oven
1,500 W

= 8,350 W

Large electric
cooker/stove
4,400 W

Electric griller
1,250 W

# Home inspection

You can help save energy in your household by doing your very own 'home-energy audit'. Room by room, count light bulbs, appliances and gadgets. Test doors and windows for draughts. Then, like a police detective, use your list of clues to figure out ways to save energy.

|  | Sitting room | Kitchen |
|---|---|---|
| total light bulbs | 12 | 8 |
| low-energy (CFL) bulbs | 11 | 0 |
| draughts detected | 2 | 1 |
| electrical appliances | 5 | 7 |
| appliances with standby | 1 | 2 |

12:00

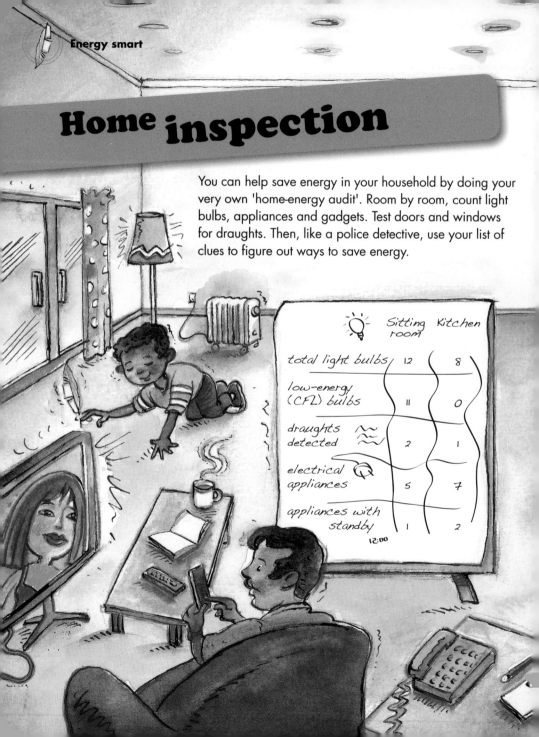

# How to make a draught excluder

Spaces under doors allow heat to flow between rooms, wasting lots of energy. You can block these draughts and keep rooms warmer by making a draught excluder out of an old long-sleeved T-shirt. Here's how:

| Cut off the sleeves | Sew the shoulder ends together | Fill with sand and T-shirt pieces | Fasten ends with rubber bands |

# See the difference

**Energy Smart**

Most of the energy you use comes from fossil fuels (coal, gas and oil). Burning these fuels to generate electricity releases carbon-dioxide gas. Carbon-dioxide is the main gas involved in global warming. So when you cut back on energy use at home, you not only reduce your power bills, you also help to save the planet.

Before you use an electrical appliance, think of an energy-saving alternative.

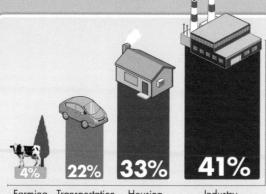

**Carbon culprits** Almost all man-made carbon-dioxide emissions come from factories, homes and vehicles – a third of these emissions come from our houses.

**Hanging out washing 0 W**; tumble dryer 4,400 W

**Unplugged microwave 0 W**; on standby 5 W

**Wearing a jumper and thick socks 0 W**; electric heater 2,400 W

**Hand-washing shirt 100 W**; washing machine 1,100 W

**CFL or low-energy bulb 30 W**; ordinary light bulb 100 W

# Scarce water

In the developed world, where water is cheap and readily available, people take it for granted. But fresh, clean water is more rare and precious than it seems. As the world's population grows, more and more water is used to supply homes, farms and factories. Unless we protect and save our water, there may soon be too little to go around.

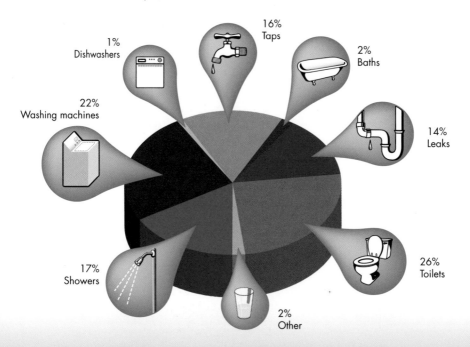

16%
Taps

1%
Dishwashers

2%
Baths

22%
Washing machines

14%
Leaks

17%
Showers

26%
Toilets

2%
Other

Where does it all go? The graph shows how much water is used, and where, around the average home.

Our world has water everywhere but less than 1 per cent of this water is fresh, clean and available.

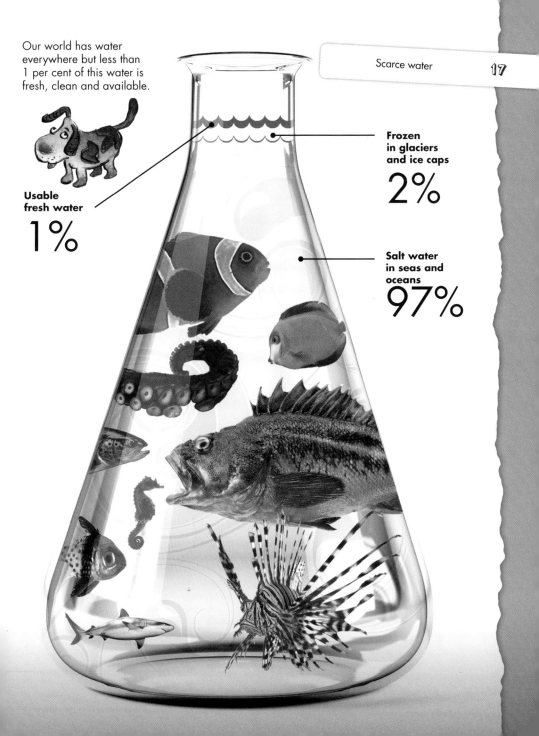

**Usable fresh water**
# 1%

**Frozen in glaciers and ice caps**
# 2%

**Salt water in seas and oceans**
# 97%

# Keep it clean

With fresh water being so precious, polluting what little we have is a truly stupid thing to do. When we treat our lakes and rivers like rubbish dumps, we not only pollute our water supplies but also do long-lasting damage to plants and wildlife. One easy way to prevent this is, of course, not to dump things in the first place. But we can also rescue wildlife and reclaim our rivers by joining organised cleanup projects and removing the rubbish that is already there.

# River rubbish

Dumped objects can damage river systems in all kinds of ways. Some rubbish can leach toxins or chemically pollute the water, making it unsafe for plants, wildlife and people. Other items can trap, injure or kill the fish, birds and insects that make their homes in the water.

Traps small fish and insects

Injures wildlife

Traps and drowns wildlife

Toxic metals pollute water

Chemical pollution

**Water wise**

# Waste not

Why work so hard to keep our water clean, then pour it down the drain? Most of the water we draw from lakes, rivers and wells is wasted and we waste more water at home than anywhere else. But a little thought can make a big difference. Do you really need a bath or will a quick shower do? Do clothes worn only once really need washing or are you just too lazy to hang them up? Think before you use!

Farms
31%

Factories
88%

Homes
91%

These three spills represent the water wasted by houses, farms and factories. Households are the biggest water wasters of all.

**Water wise**

# Match and catch

Where can water be caught and recycled, instead of drained away?

To save even more water at home, we can go beyond just using less. We can also reuse water from cooking, cleaning and washing – or even top up our supplies by collecting free rainwater outside. But how and where do we catch and recycle? Try this water-recycling picture quiz; match each water source with the best way to catch it and the best way to use it.

✿ ◐ ▽
(to cool)
✿ ◐ ▽
✿ ◐ ▽
✿ ◐ ▽
Answers

Now, which container will work best for collecting it?

How can we put our free, recycled water to good use?

# Test yourself

People of different continents and countries use very different amounts of water in daily life. The average American or European uses more than 300 litres (66 gallons) of water a day for drinking, washing, cooking and cleaning. Yet in sub-Saharan Africa, people are forced to survive on 14 litres (3 gallons) or less. If you really had to, could you do the same?

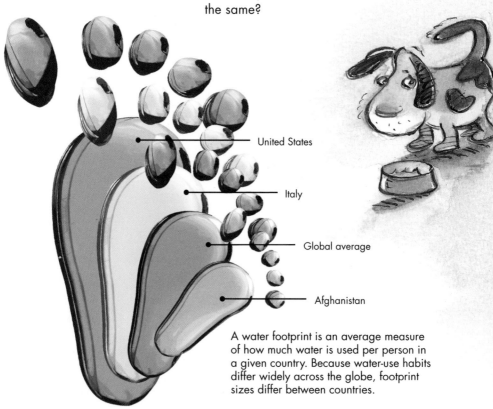

United States

Italy

Global average

Afghanistan

A water footprint is an average measure of how much water is used per person in a given country. Because water-use habits differ widely across the globe, footprint sizes differ between countries.

Which daily activities could you skip
to save water, and which are essential?

When there is little water
left to drink, desert
peoples may suck
pebbles to stave off thirst!

Brushing teeth is too
important to skip but in
some countries people
clean their teeth with a twig!

ONLY 14 L (3 GALLONS)

How about wearing socks
and shirts for an extra day
before washing them?

Eating raw vegetables
instead of cooking them
saves panfuls of water.

Flushing is hard to avoid
but 'if it's yellow, let it
mellow' and save a
cistern full of water.

Could you save water
by wiping your face
with a damp flannel
instead of washing it?

# See the difference
## Water wise

Taking small, simple steps to save water in and around your home can make a huge difference to your household water use. Saving just a few litres each day can add up to hundreds of litres over the course of a year. If the whole family gets involved, you can save thousands of litres or gallons of water per year – enough to fill two or three houses from floor to ceiling.

Turning off the shower while you soap up saves 75 litres (16 gallons) per person per day or 27,375 litres (6,020 gallons) in a year.

Turning off the tap while you brush your teeth saves 15 litres (3 gallons) per person each day and 5,475 litres (1200 gallons) a year.

Watering plants with recycled cooking water or rainwater saves 20 litres (4 gallons) per family per day or 7,300 litres (1,600 gallons) a year.

Washing vegetables in a small basin, rather than under a running tap, saves 10 litres (2 gallons) per family per day and 3,650 litres (800 gallons) per family per year.

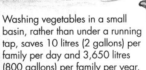

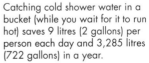

Catching cold shower water in a bucket (while you wait for it to run hot) saves 9 litres (2 gallons) per person each day and 3,285 litres (722 gallons) in a year.

# Eat local

Many people buy food in big supermarkets, which are convenient and offer a wide choice. But supermarkets usually get their goods from farmers in distant places and the further your food has to travel, the more energy is used to transport it. Buying local foods in season from a farmers' market helps cut down on these food miles and saves the energy that would otherwise be used to transport them.

# One great reason to eat by season

Whenever you eat summer fruits in winter or winter vegetables in summer, you should realise that your food has travelled hundreds of miles to get to you. Try to buy fruits and vegetables that are in season – you'll find they taste better, too!.

SNOWFLAKES

TROPICAL FRUIT

200 km
(125 miles)

500 km
(310 miles)

# Organic food

Most of the 'fresh' foods found in your local supermarket are farmed using chemicals to make crops grow, and to keep weeds and pests at bay. These fertilisers, herbicides and pesticides can damage our environment, our wildlife and our bodies. But organic foods are different. Organic farmers use natural manure or compost instead of chemical fertiliser, pull up weeds by hand and pair-up crop plants so that they help each other to grow and stay pest free.

## Bug blitz

Some, but not all, of the pesticide will fall in the right place.

Using aeroplanes to spray fields with chemical pesticides is a cheap and easy way of killing crop pests. But aerial spraying can easily miss the target. The spray may damage nearby fields, forests and wildlife or contaminate the surface waters of rivers, lakes and ponds.

Compost releases nitrogen slowly into the soil.

 **Green food**

# Grow your own

Buying organic fruits and vegetables is a good way to help the environment. But you can't get any fresher than food you grow yourself! It's easy and fun to grow your own vegetables and herbs, and you don't need a huge garden to do it. You can grow your plants in pots or tubs, on a balcony, on a windowsill or on the pavement outside your house. Give it a try!

Tomatoes love recycled water from scrubbed vegetables.

Weeding and tending your veggie patch can be fun!

Some vegetables are easier to grow than others. These four are simple to care for and extremely good for you.

**Cherry tomatoes:** high in vitamins A, C and K

**Carrots:** contain fibre plus vitamins, A, C and B6

**Lettuce:** high in fibre, calcium and iron

**Radishes:** low in fat, high in vitamin C

Fresh herbs can be clipped for delicious recipes.

 **Green food**

# Meat choices

The average American or European diet contains a lot of meat from cattle and sheep. But raising livestock takes lots of grain for animal feed, which in turn requires lots of land and water for growing it. So eating too much meat can actually affect the world's food supplies as well as the environment.

Producing 1 kg (2.2 lb) of beef uses lots of grain and huge amounts of water.

It takes vast amounts of grain-feed to produce just 1 kg (2.2 lb) of lamb.

10,000 L (2,200 gallons) water

Hungry pigs mean lots of grain and water are needed for pork production, too.

4,800 L (1,055 gallons) water

6 kg (13 lb) grain

Raising chickens uses less grain and water than other animals but is still costly.

3,500 L (770 gallons) water

2 kg (4.4 lb) grain

Growing 1 kg (2.2 lb) of potatoes or other veggies requires very little water and no grain at all.

500 L (110 gallons) water

0 kg (0 lb) grain

Cows and sheep burp and fart a lot. Their burps contain methane gas, which contributes to global warming!

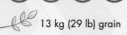 13 kg (29 lb) grain

100,000 L (22,000 gallons) water

1 kg (2.2 lb) beef

21 kg (46 lb) grain

1kg (2.2 lb) lamb

1 kg (2.2 lb) pork

1 kg (2.2 lb) chicken

1 kg (2.2 lb) potatoes

# See the difference
### Green food

Being aware of what you eat and how it affects the environment can make a big difference to your life. Growing your own food and buying organic produce will leave you feeling happy and healthy every time you eat. Happy that you have helped to protect all the water sources, soils, wild plants and wildlife in your environment. And healthy from all that lovely, fresh, chemical-free green food!

Choosing 'greener' foods protects both the environment and your health. After all – do you really want to be eating chemical pesticides every day?

 **Getting around**

# Short trips

More than half of all car journeys are very short ones of less than 5 km (3 miles). These short trips include commuting to work, shopping and dropping children off at schools. Millions of cars make these short trips every day. But in stop-and-start traffic, cars on short journeys use more fuel and release more climate-damaging carbon dioxide gas. So for trips like these, do you really need to go by car at all?

3 KM (2 MILES)

1 KM (²/₃ MILE)

5 KM (3 MILES)

| | Where to? | How far? | How many passengers? |
|---|---|---|---|
| Monday | school | 3 km (2 miles) | 2 |
| Tuesday | rugby | 5½ km (3½ miles) | 4 |
| Wednesday | shops | 1 km (²/₃ mile) | 3 |
| Thursday | | | |
| Friday | | | |
| Saturday | | | |
| Sunday | | | |

# Keeping a car log

One good way of becoming more aware of how much you use the family car is to keep a car log. For each journey, note how far you travelled, how many people were in the car and how often you made that trip in a week. You may be surprised at the results!

# Curb that car

If you find that you are making a lot of short trips, you can save on fuel, energy and harmful carbon-dioxide emissions by thinking about other ways to travel. Taking the bus or sharing car trips with friends lowers the energy and emissions per person. Better yet – cycling, skateboarding and walking (on your own, or with other kids and adults in 'walking trains') release no emissions at all!

# Low emissions, NO emissions

Different forms of transport release different amounts of climate-damaging carbon dioxide and some release almost none at all. If you count all the time you spend waiting for a lift, travelling and parking, some of these 'no-emissions' options are almost as quick as driving over short distances.

On a skateboard you can travel 1 km (two-thirds of a mile) in 6 minutes and 3 km (2 miles) in 18 minutes.

By cycling, it takes 3 minutes to travel 1 km (two-thirds of a mile) and only 9 minutes to travel 3 km (2 miles).

You can walk 1 km (two-thirds of a mile) in 10 minutes and 3 km (2 miles) in 32 minutes.

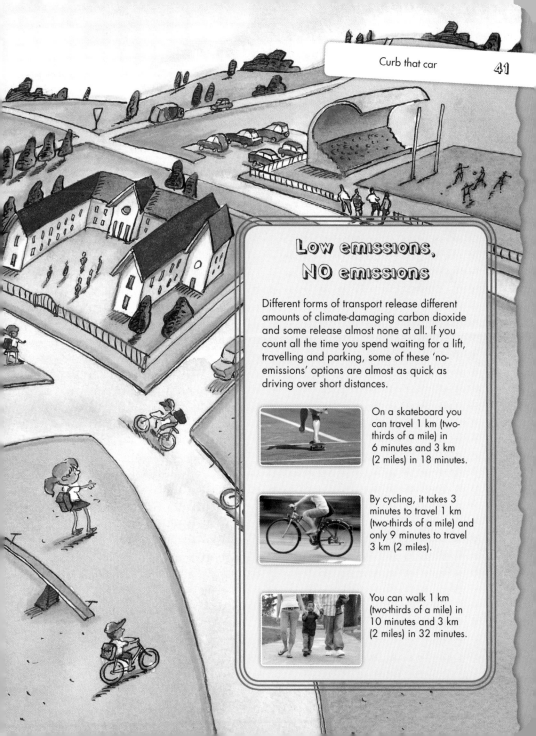

# Long trips

If you can avoid longer trips it is better for the environment. For the journeys you can't skip, choosing how you travel can still make a big difference. Cars and aeroplanes use the most fuel and release the most carbon-dioxide per passenger. So how about going by bus or train instead? It might take a little longer but you can help save the planet and enjoy the journey as you go!

Aeroplanes release tonnes of gases high into the atmosphere, where they do the worst damage.

Cars and trucks burn through as much fuel per person as aeroplanes.

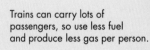

Trains can carry lots of passengers, so use less fuel and produce less gas per person.

LESS CO$_2$

1½ clouds
3 nozzles

1 cloud
2 nozzles

LEAST FUEL

Coaches and buses use less fuel per person than trains, so are even kinder to the atmosphere.

Every year, millions of holidaymakers fly thousands of kilometres in search of fun in the sun. We can limit the pollution and the damage this causes by carefully choosing how (and how far) we travel.

**BIG EMITTER**

21 clouds
11 nozzles

**BIG GUZZLER**

13 clouds
11 nozzles

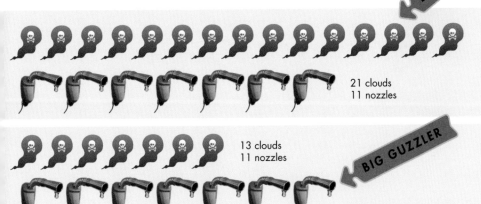

Each gas cloud in the picture represents 10 kg (22 lb) of carbon-dioxide gas released per person

Each petrol pump in the picture represents 3 L (0.66 gallons) of petrol used per person

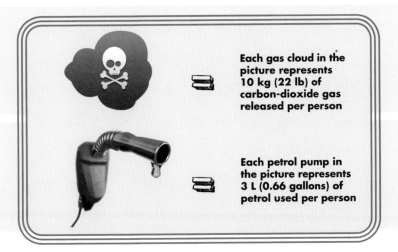

# See the difference

### Getting around

In developed countries, most cars carry just one or two people, and fewer than 30 per cent of children who live within 1.5 km (1 mile) of school walk there. But every person who chooses to walk, cycle, car pool or take the bus removes one car from the road. And the more cars we get off the road, the more energy we save and the less damage we do to the atmosphere.

Traffic jams spew tons of carbon dioxide as engines idle and cars inch their way forwards.

Crowded 'people jams' may be uncomfortable but release little carbon dioxide – except what comes from heavy breathing!

# Save for later

Recycling used things to save the materials they are made from is a good habit. But reusing whole items instead of buying new ones is even better because it also saves the energy that would have been used to recycle them. Older people often keep a drawer full of scrap objects to save money. You can do the same thing to save money, energy and the environment.

Used wrapping paper

Gift ribbon

# Start your squirreling

Your parents or grandparents may squirrel away bits of string, ribbon and wrapping paper but your own 'save for later' box could include much, much more. You could collect paper used on one side, old CD cases, files, folders, binders, batteries – whatever you can think of.

Brown paper

Paper clips

Used string

Pencil stubs

Elastic bands

Used envelopes

# Reuse... or refuse

Once you have assembled your collection of reusable items, it is time to put them to work. You could turn an old CD case into a photo frame. You could make filing trays from old cereal boxes to file your homework or you could make a new notepad out of used paper and card. Time to get creative! If something cannot be reused, think twice before bringing it home.

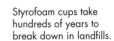

Plastic water bottles are recyclable, but why not just drink tap water?

Metallic balloons cannot be reused and don't break down naturally.

Styrofoam cups take hundreds of years to break down in landfills.

Plastic bags are often too flimsy to reuse and are costly to recycle.

Plastic food wrap is harmful to the environment and is usually unnecessary.

## Make your own notebook

1 Stack some sheets of used paper with the used sides facing each other and staple the sheets together.
2 Put two pieces of thick card on the top and bottom of the stack of paper.
3 Punch three holes at even distances from the left edge, thread ribbon through the holes, tie, and you're done!

# Recycle

Everything we throw away has to end up somewhere, and most of it ends up in huge underground dumps called landfills. Every year, hundreds of millions of tonnes of rubbish rot away in landfills, damaging the environment and atmosphere. Yet most of this waste could be recycled instead. So if you can't reuse it, recycle it. Flatten boxes, rinse tins, remove tops from bottles, sort out recyclable plastics and compost any food scraps that your pets don't want. Do it right, and you'll have almost nothing left to dump!

This diagram shows the percentage of recyclable items found in a typical landfill. About 92 per cent of our waste could be recycled or composted.

Metal
9%

Garden waste
18%

Paper
41%

Food
9%

Plastic
7%

Glass
8%

plastic

compost

# New from old

In the United States, most drink cans are made from aluminium. In Europe and Asia, about 55 per cent of drink cans are made from steel. Both steel and aluminium can be recycled, which reduces the amount of carbon dioxide released into the atmosphere. Every year, billions of cans around the world end up dumped in landfill sites or are left littering the landscape. Recycling cans reduces waste and saves energy and materials.

## 13 billion cans

In the UK, 13 billion steel cans are used every year. Stacked on top of each other, this many cans would reach to the Moon and back... twice over.

## Remaking

Wood, paper, glass, plastics and metals can easily be extracted from rubbish and remade into new objects.

This bicycle does not look anything like the 500 steel cans it came from.

Recycling one plastic bottle saves enough energy to power a 60 W light bulb for 6 hours.

Recycling paper can cut the volume of rubbish sent to landfills by 50 per cent.

Recycling one tonne of glass saves 225 kg (495 lb) of carbon dioxide.

New picture frames can be made from recycled wood, paper or cardboard.

# Compost

Many gardeners build compost heaps to help fertilise their plants. Bacteria and fungi in these heaps break down organic materials to make nitrogen-rich fertiliser, which helps plants to grow. But did you know that over a quarter of all household waste can be composted? Food scraps, eggshells, hair clippings and more can be piled on and broken down, saving on waste and keeping your garden healthy at the same time.

You can start an open compost heap in the garden or build your heap inside a special composting bin.

## IN

Compost heaps love nutrient-rich grass cuttings, weeds, pet hair, tea bags, vegetable peelings, rotten fruit and dust from hoover bags. Add shredded newspaper and water between layers.

# Wriggly recyclers

If you don't have space for a large compost heap, you can build a small worm farm instead. Worms gobble many types of rubbish. Kept in a soil-filled tub, they will happily munch on paper and food scraps to make compost.

OUT

Fats, oils, cooked food, pet litter and pesticide-coated plants should be left out of your compost, as they create bad smells, attract rodents and may cause illness or disease when the compost is used.

Shredded newspaper helps the breakdown of compost.

# See the difference

**Trash or treasure**

In developed countries, the average person dumps 2–3 kilograms (4–6 lb) of rubbish each day. Worldwide, this adds up to millions of tonnes of rubbish every year. This waste material is dumped in landfills, piled in mountainous heaps or burned in incinerators, wasting land, polluting soils and groundwater, and releasing climate-altering gases into the atmosphere. Cutting back on waste disposal can help us to avoid these problems, if only we make the effort.

**Landfills** could be returned to grass.

If we all recycled or composted every piece of waste that we could, the effects would be massive.

As landfills rot, they release methane, which is a greenhouse gas twenty times more powerful and damaging than carbon dioxide.

**Rubbish mountains** could be cut in half.

**Incinerators** would release far less carbon dioxide.

# Do you **need it?**

In developed countries, we can go a bit shopping-crazy at times. In the USA, for example, the average person spends 24 minutes a day shopping for new things. All these things have to be made somewhere, from something. Eventually, all this new stuff ends up in the rubbish, doing damage to the planet. So before you work so hard at recycling and reusing, just think – do you really need to buy it in the first place?

Try going for a whole day without buying anything at all – it might not be as easy as you think!

# Shop or swap

## Smarter choices

Single-use batteries contain toxic chemicals.

One rechargeable battery can do the job of 1,000 ordinary batteries.

Shop for reusable and recyclable things rather than those that are used once and tossed away. Even something as simple as a battery can make a big difference. Each rechargeable battery can be used again and again before being discarded. This is important for the environment as batteries dumped in landfills can leak mercury and arsenic into surrounding soils.

# Shop green

It takes thousands of tonnes of material and a vast amount of energy to make, package and transport all the books, CDs and DVDs we buy each year, and most are thrown away after being used just once or twice. So why not save on energy and materials by borrowing or renting them instead? Check out your local public library – you may be surprised at its collection of music CDs and film DVDs, as well as all the books you're ever likely to read.

Borrowing and 'virtual' shopping through downloads are much 'greener' (and cheaper!) ways to get new films and music.

Your local library is a great resource for books, CDs and films.

**No pirates!**
Download-shopping is good but downloading 'free' pirated music and films is a crime!

# Swap club

Most of us own things we don't need or want any more. But when the time comes to get rid of your 'old and useless' stuff, remember that swapping and reusing is even better for the environment than recycling – as it uses no new energy or materials.

Try trading unwanted books, toys, films and music with friends or family members. Even if nobody wants to swap, don't just throw these things out. Take them to a charity shop instead. The shop can sell your old stuff for a good cause, and someone, somewhere will be happy to reuse it.

# Giving good deeds

The things you buy for people often end up lost, broken or forgotten, but the thoughtful things you do for people can be appreciated and remembered long afterwards. What could you offer? Could you wash someone's car or tidy their garden? How about teaching a younger brother or sister to ride a bike or play a new game?

Dear Grandpa,
Happy 70th Birthday!
My special present to you is a promise to mow your lawn and weed your garden for a year.
Love from,
Daniel

Dear Mum, I grew these herbs myself

Dear Dad, I made this paperweight for you

# Perfect presents

You can make holidays and birthdays greener – and happier – by giving home-made gifts instead of buying new things. You could make a present for someone from scratch or give them something special of your own. Better still, you can give good deeds by offering to help people out in special ways. Presents like these are not only better for the planet, they are also unique and wonderful for those who receive them.

Dear Fin
I know you
have always
wanted my
scooter

# See the difference
## Shop or swap

In the USA alone, over 100,000 CDs and DVDs are thrown away every month – enough to make a 12,000-metre (39,000-foot) tower, taller than Mount Everest! You can help cut this down to size.

The way you choose to enjoy your books, music, films and electronics can make a massive difference to our planet. Making new electronic hardware and storage media takes a lot of energy, water and raw materials, and also produces harmful chemicals and atmospheric pollution. Swapping, second-hand shopping, downloading and borrowing will help save on all of these. And getting others to follow your example can turn one small step into a huge change.

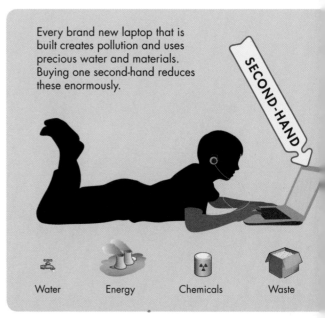

Every brand new laptop that is built creates pollution and uses precious water and materials. Buying one second-hand reduces these enormously.

SECOND-HAND

Water    Energy    Chemicals    Waste

**4 people** with second-hand laptops save 132,000 L (29,000 gallons) of water, 9,200 kWh of energy, 7 kg (16 lb) of toxic chemicals, 255 kg (560 lb) of waste.

**30 people** with second-hand laptops save 996,450 L (219,000 gallons) of water, 69,000 kWh of energy, 55 kg (120 lb) of toxic chemicals, 1,910 kg (4,200 lb) of waste.

**500 people** with second-hand laptops save 16,607,500 L (3,650,000 gallons) of water, 1,150,000 kWh of energy, 910 kg (2,000 lb) of toxic chemicals, 31,800 kg (70,000 lb) of waste.

# Tree watch

Most people don't even notice trees, let alone appreciate what the trees are doing for them. But you can keep watch and take notice of all they do. Trees provide shade and shelter from sun, wind and rain, and their trunks absorb sound from noisy roads. Trees provide food and a home for birds, insects and other animals. Their leaves feed the soil and their roots help to protect it. They give out oxygen and take in carbon dioxide, which helps keep Earth's climate in balance.

## Where did all the trees go?

About half of the world's felled trees are burned as fuel for heating and cooking. Another third are used to make wood for building things. One-sixth of felled trees are smashed into wood pulp and made into paper, in pulp mills like this one.

**Check your local trees each month and keep a log.**

How many are there within a square block of your home?

When do they flower?

What colours are the flowers?

Do they lose their leaves in winter?

Can you see how large their root systems are?

What animals, birds and insects can you see?

Do you see any damage? Is there any rubbish around the roots? Can you clear it up?

# Paper trail

You may think you use very little paper and cardboard at home but if you stop and look around, you will be astonished by how many paper products surround you. Books, magazines and notepads are easy enough to spot but try going room-by-room around your home, and you will find paper towels, toilet rolls, leaflets, letters, tissues, pictures, postcards, printouts and much, much more!

Wiping with reusable rags and handkerchiefs is far better than wasting paper towels and tissues.

# Recycle it

Every year, so much paper is thrown away that, if you stacked it all up, you could build a wall 3.5 metres (12 ft) high, right across the USA, from California to New York! Recycling even some of this paper waste would save the millions of trees, billions of litres of water and billions of kilowatts of energy that are used to create it.

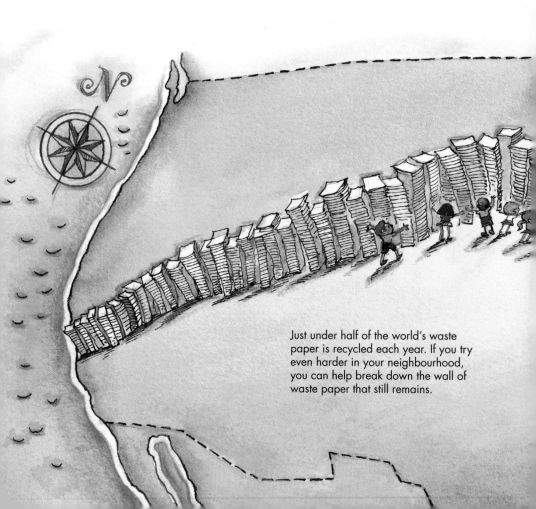

Just under half of the world's waste paper is recycled each year. If you try even harder in your neighbourhood, you can help break down the wall of waste paper that still remains.

Keep a box of paper used on one side only, reuse old envelopes or make new gift cards from the unused parts of cards you've received.

 **Save the trees**

# How paper is recycled

First, paper is collected from recycling centres and sorted into different paper types. Then it's fed into a pulping machine, which adds water and chemicals before chopping the paper into a mushy pulp. Next, the pulp is filtered and washed by screening and deinking machines, which remove ink and nasty bits like staples and glue. Then the pulp is beaten and more water is added. Finally, the mix is sprayed on to screens, dried and wound on to giant rolls – ready to start all over again.

# Paper transformed!

Recycled and recovered paper pulp is not just used to make more paper. It can also be transformed into any one of over 5,000 paper-related products. These include toilet paper, tea bags, pizza boxes, pet litter, labels, lampshades, disposable nappies, drinking straws, bookmarks, bandages and thousands of other things!

# See the difference

**Save the trees**

If everyone you knew recycled all their paper, together you could save enormous numbers of trees from being chopped down. Recycling on your own, you can save enough paper in a year to equal four whole trees – four trees that can be left to grow, rather than being cut down, mashed and pulped, to make new paper. Get others involved and you could save many, many more trees!

**Your entire school**, recycling all its paper every year, would save an entire forest!

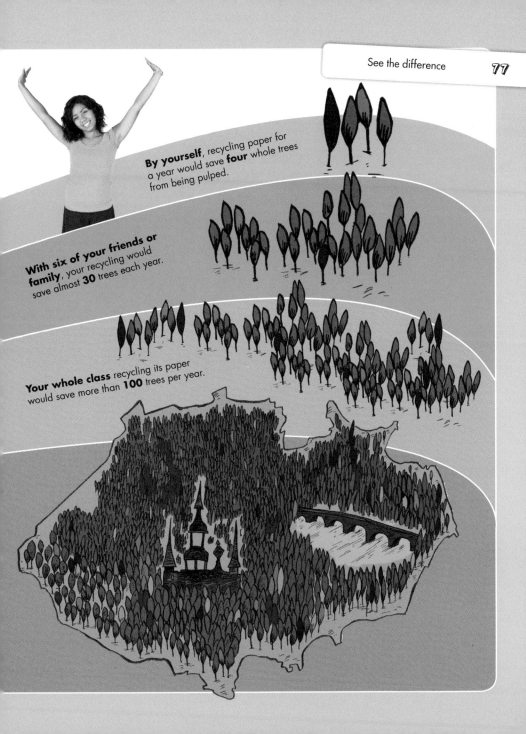

**By yourself**, recycling paper for a year would save **four** whole trees from being pulped.

**With six of your friends or family**, your recycling would save almost **30** trees each year.

**Your whole class** recycling its paper would save more than **100** trees per year.

# Rogue rubbish

Sadly, some people treat their local beaches like rubbish dumps and the ocean like a giant litter bin. The rubbish they toss may sink out of sight but it does untold harm to sea creatures as they become choked, poisoned or ensnared by it later on. So take your own rubbish home, pick up litter where you can and help keep the seaside safe for all animals.

Organised clean-up

Turtles can choke to death on plastic bags and other rubbish.

Dolphins are often trapped and drowned in discarded nets.

**Wildlife watch**

Feathers, shells, skins and other animal trinkets may look pretty but they look far better on the beautiful animals they came from.

Don't buy carved and decorated horns, tusks and teeth.

A bag made from the skin of a snake or crocodile means a reptile has been killed.

Exotic shells, sponges and corals should be left where they belong.

# Leave it there

Many birds, mammals and shellfish have been hunted to extinction for their feathers, furs, tusks, teeth, horns, skins and shells. Many more species are becoming endangered as this hunting goes on. Every time we pick up or purchase an animal souvenir like this, we encourage the destruction of animals and their fragile habitats. So the next time you take a trip, bring back pictures and memories – but leave the animals where they are.

Taking pictures of exotic plants and animals is a harmless way to bring back memories.

Rare bird feathers look better on live birds.

## Leave and let live

Though you may not realise it at the time, sometimes collecting can be the same as killing. Picking pretty wildflowers can kill rare plants and there may still be crabs or shellfish living in that shell you picked up on the beach.

# Helping out

With a little effort, you can create a safe haven for local wildlife in your very own neighbourhood. Many neighbourhoods have spare land or an undeveloped area that could be turned into a beautiful, animal-friendly community garden. Just get your neighbours together to plan it and get to work! You can also encourage and support wildlife in your own back garden with animal feeders, bird baths and nesting boxes.

Where could you plant a garden in your neighborhood?

Creating a new garden can be hugely rewarding, and working together with friends, family and neighbours can be great fun, too!

Give an owl a home in your garden and it will give you something fascinating to watch and will keep rodents at bay.

A bird bath will bring lots of beautiful birds into your garden to drink and bathe.

Bats, roosting in a bat box, will munch and destroy lots of pesky mosquitoes.

A community garden brings birds, bees, butterflies and beauty.

# Plant native

If you want to create a truly Earth-friendly garden, it's very important to grow plants that are naturally found in your area. Native trees, plants and wildflowers are not only easier to care for than exotic or foreign species, they are also essential for supporting animal food chains and ecosystems. So avoid the exotic and go for native and natural.

## Natural fit

Many birds and insects depend upon local plant species for food and shelter. Birds may pick particular tree species for their berries and branches, while bees, butterflies and other insects search for nectar in specific flowers.

# See the difference

For all the plant and animal species the world has lost to hunting and habitat destruction, a good many have actually been brought back from the brink of extinction. Trees, flowers, birds, butterflies and many more species have been saved by bans on hunting and efforts to conserve and restore their natural habitats. So support local nature reserves, care for native plants and animals, make space for local wildlife and help make your world a better place.

**Black-footed ferrets** were nearly wiped out by poisoning and habitat destruction but, with better protection, are making a comeback.

**Green turtles** were almost hunted to extinction but are now being protected in many countries.

**American alligators** are still endangered but are now protected from hide hunters.

**Queen Alexandra birdwing butterflies**, the largest butterflies in the world, have survived extinction but are still endangered.

The prehistoric **Wollemi Pine**, known as 'the dinosaur tree', was thought to be extinct. Then, in 1994, it was found growing wild in Australia. It is now being grown and replanted worldwide.

**Birds of paradise** are no longer endangered, thanks to hunting bans in Papua New Guinea.

**African elephant** numbers are recovering because of a ban on ivory hunting.

# My carbon footprint

A carbon footprint is a measure of how much impact your lifestyle has on the environment. It is created by estimating how much carbon dioxide your everyday activities release into the atmosphere each year. By calculating the size of your footprint and taking steps to reduce it, you and your family can cut your carbon-dioxide emissions and help with the global battle against climate change.

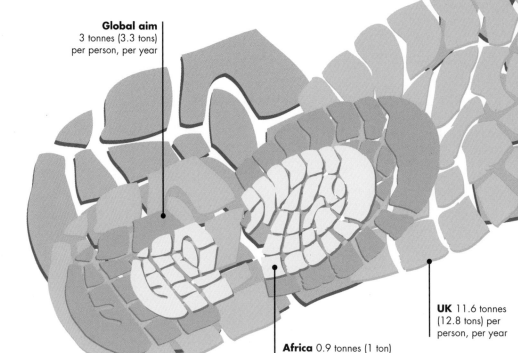

**Global aim**
3 tonnes (3.3 tons)
per person, per year

**UK** 11.6 tonnes
(12.8 tons) per
person, per year

**Africa** 0.9 tonnes (1 ton)
per person, per year

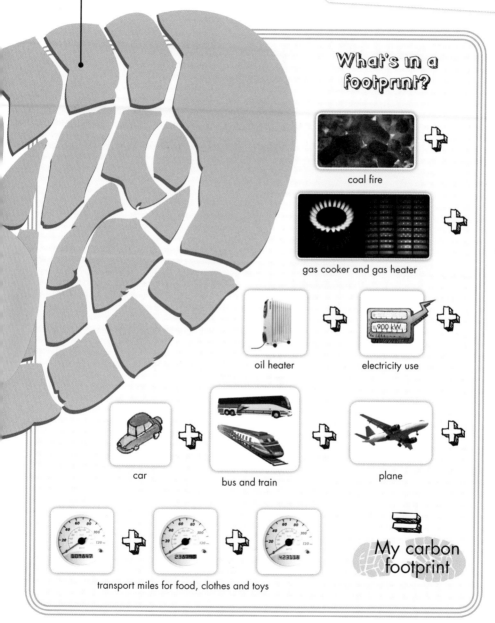

US 25.9 tonnes (28.5 tons) per person, per year

What's in a footprint?

coal fire

gas cooker and gas heater

oil heater

electricity use

car

bus and train

plane

transport miles for food, clothes and toys

My carbon footprint

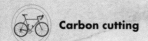

# My carbon offsets

Carbon offsets are activities that help to make up for – or offset – the amount of greenhouse gases your daily activities release into the atmosphere. You can create your own offsets by doing 'good' things to make up for your 'bad' energy use. Turn it into a game, where energy-wasting activities (shown here on the red cards) score minus points, while energy-saving ones (on the green cards) score plus points. For every red card activity you do, aim to get your score back to zero by doing green ones.

Trashing one glass bottle

-3

Drinking plastic-bottled water

-6

Hanging out washing in the sun

+15

Recycling one glass bottle

+4

+1

Using a CFL bulb for a day

Cycling a
short journey

Tumble-drying
clothes when the
sun is shining

Drinking
tap water

Using an ordinary light
bulb for a day

Playing a non-electronic
game for an hour

Driving a
short journey

Playing console
or computer games
for an hour

# find out more

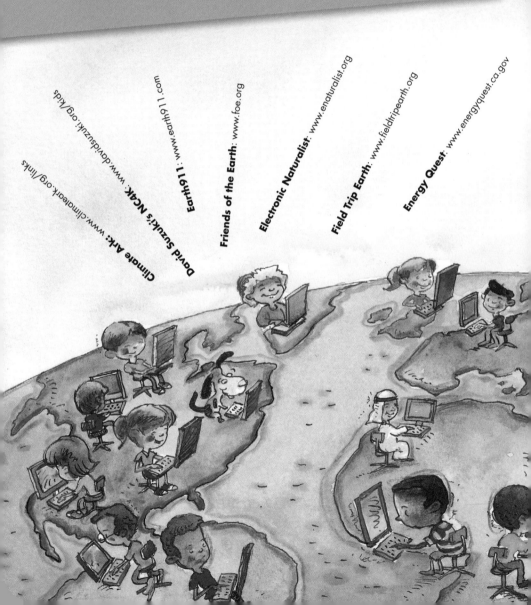

Climate Ark: www.climateark.org/links

David Suzuki's NC4K: www.davidsuzuki.org/kids

Earth911: www.earth911.com

Friends of the Earth: www.foe.org

Electronic Naturalist: www.enaturalist.org

Field Trip Earth: www.fieldtripearth.org

Energy Quest: www.energyquest.ca.gov

The Greens: www.meetthegreens.org

Planet Slayer: www.abc.net.au/science/planetslayer

Earth's Endangered Creatures: www.earthsendangered.org

Kid's Planet: www.kidsplanet.org

I Buy Different (WWF): www.ibuydifferent.com

Recycle City: www.epa.gov/recyclecity

Nature's Best Photography for Students: www.naturesbeststudents.com

Green Squad: www.nrdc.org/greensquad

EcoKids Planet Protectors: www.ecokids.ca/pub/kids_home.cfm

EPA Student Center: www.epa.gov/students

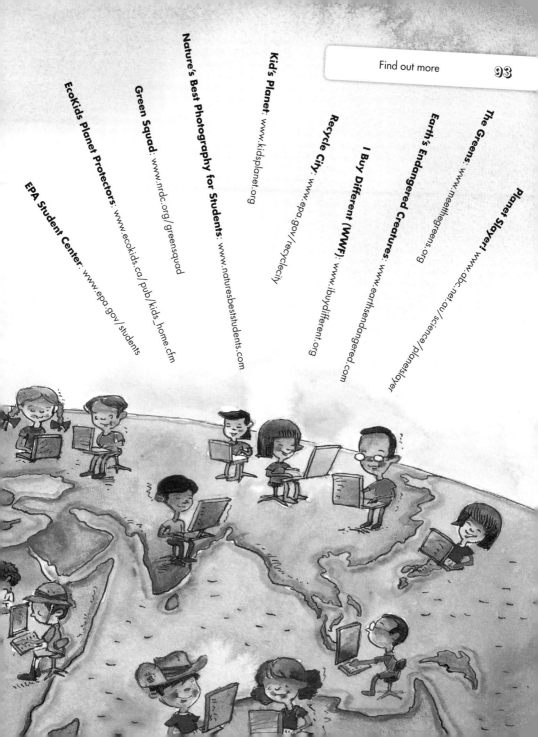

# Glossary

**carbon dioxide** The main greenhouse gas involved in global warming and climate change. Carbon dioxide is released into the atmosphere when we burn fossil fuels for heating, transport or to create electricity.

**carbon footprint** A measure of how much impact a person, organisation or activity has on the environment. A carbon footprint is calculated by adding up greenhouse-gas emissions and expressed in tonnes of carbon dioxide per year.

**carbon offset** An activity which makes up for, or 'offsets', greenhouse-gas emissions made elsewhere. Carbon offsets help to reduce your net gas emissions.

**CFL bulb**: Compact Fluorescent Lamp, a type of low-energy lightbulb that produces the same amount of light as a standard bulb but uses less electricity and lasts 8–15 times longer.

**climate change** A long-term change in global weather patterns and temperatures with both natural and man-made causes.

**composting** Converting organic matter, such as leaves, grass cuttings and manure, into a nutritious soil fertiliser for plants.

**ecosystem** A natural web of plants, animals, bacteria and other living organisms, which interact with each other and their environment in one living system.

**emissions** Substances, usually gases, released into the atmosphere by factories, machines or living creatures.

**endangered species** Plant or animal species at risk of extinction, usually as a result of human activities.

**extinction** The dying out of an entire species of plant, animal or organism.

**food miles** A measure of how far an item of food has travelled between where it was produced and where it is bought or consumed.

**global warming** An increase in the Earth's average temperature over time, which leads to long-term changes in climate and weather.

**greenhouse gases** Gases found in the Earth's atmosphere, which trap heat and warm the planet. Man-made increases in greenhouse-gas emissions are thought to be the main cause of global warming.

**habitat** The natural environment of a living plant, animal or organism.

**herbicide** A substance, usually man-made, used for killing plants or weeds.

**incinerator** A large furnace used for burning trash or garbage.

**kWh** A kilowatt hour is the amount of power (in kilowatts) used by an electrical device or system in one hour.

**landfill** An underground pit or low area of land built up by dumping rubbish or solid waste.

**leaching** Process by which water or other liquids filter down through soils or porous materials.

**methane** A greenhouse gas found in the atmosphere. Methane is at least 20 times more powerful than carbon dioxide in its effect on global warming.

**native** A plant, animal or other organism found naturally in a particular place or region.

**nature reserve** A park or other area used to protect and preserve native plants and animals.

**nitrogen** A natural element and an invisible, odourless gas, which makes up about 80% of the air we breathe. Nitrogen is important for plant growth and is a key ingredient in fertilisers.

**nutrient** A source or substance that gives nourishment and helps living things to grow.

**organic farming** A type of farming that avoids the use of chemical fertilisers, pesticides, herbicides or food additives.

**organic material** Matter that has come from an organism that was once alive, such as a plant or animal.

**pesticide** A substance, usually a man-made chemical, used to protect plants from insects and other pests.

**pulp** Wood or paper reduced to a wet, soft mush by mechanical or chemical treatment, during the process of recycling.

**recycling** Collecting and treating waste materials so that they can be reused.

**standby power** The electrical power still being drawn from a plug or outlet when a device is left in standby mode.

**watts** A measure of power, often electrical, calculated by multiplying current by voltage.

**worm farm** A tub or box filled with worms and organic waste. The worms eat the waste, to produce nutrient-rich fertiliser for gardens.

# Index

# Credits

The publisher thanks Jo Rudd for the index.

Key t=top; l=left; r=right; tl=top left; tr=top right; c=centre;
bl=bottom left; br=bottom right

**Front cover** GI; **Back cover** Lloyd Foye,
Sarah Norton; **Spine** iS;

### Photographs
iS=iStockphoto; GI=Getty Images; SH=Shutterstock
6bc iS; 8bc iS; 10–11tc GI, cr SH, all others iS; 17c SH, iS;
22–3 iS; 24bl SH; 33tc iS; 34–5 iS; 37tl iS; 40–1tl, cr iS;
42–3 iS; 45tr, tl iS; 47tl iS; 48c GI; all others iS; 50tl iS;

52–3c GI, all others iS; 54–5 iS and SH; 57tl iS;
61cr SH; all others iS; 63tl iS; 65tc iS; 66–7 iS, 68–9 iS;
71tl iS; 75tl iS; 76bl SH, all others iS; 77tl iS; 79t GI;
tl Ron Prendergast; 81bl iS; 83t iS; 84b iS; 86–7cl GI,
tl SH, all others iS; 88–9cl GI, all others iS, 90tl iS

### Illustrations
John Bull 87tc; Dan Cole/The Art Agency 87bl;
Gabrielle Green 15tl; Sarah Horne 51tc, 52tl, 74–5c,
77, 95br; Malcolm Godwin/Moonrunner Design 42cl;
Sarah Norton 16bc, 30tr, 35br, 52c, 53tr, 68–9;
Lionel Portier 21tl, 30bc, 66–7